Contents

When do we use these things to make **light**?

What other things make **light**?

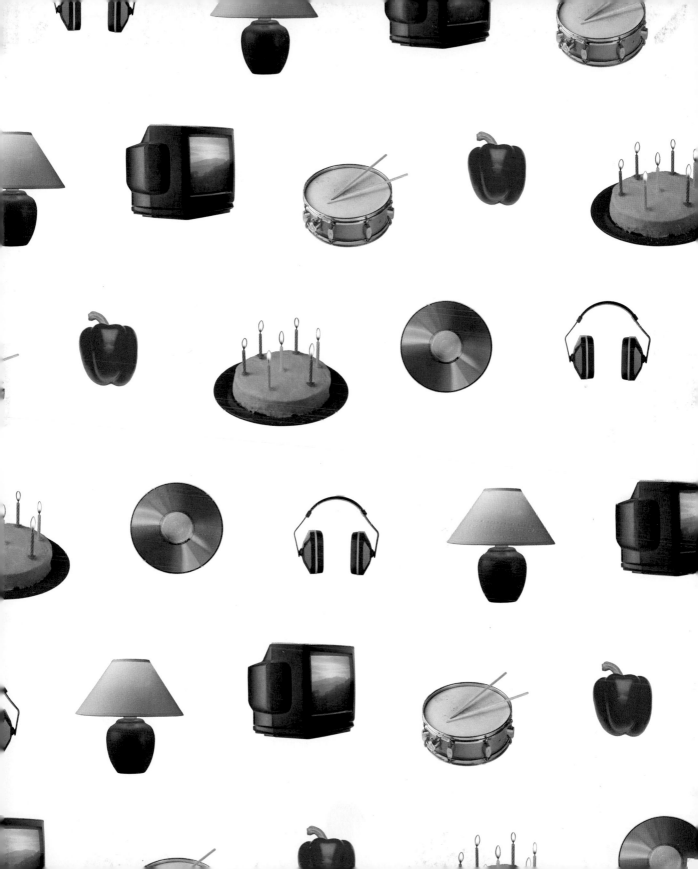

FIND OUT ABOUT

light and sound

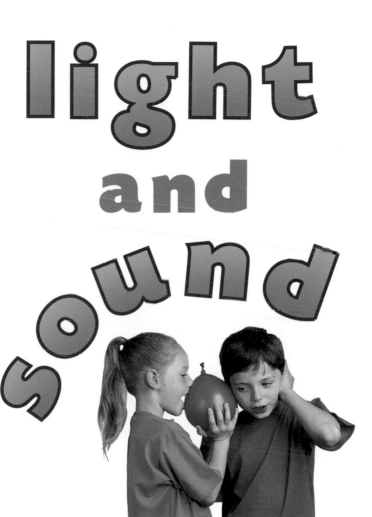

David Palmer

BBC

© **David Palmer / BBC Education 1994**

Reprinted 1997

BBC Education
201 Wood Lane
London W12 7TS

ISBN 0 563 39625 3

Editor: Christina Digby
Designer: Claire Robertson
Picture research: Helen Taylor
Consultant: Steve Pollock
Series consultant: Mary Hoffman
Educational advisers: Su Hurrell, Samina Miller
Photographer: Simon Pugh
Illustrator: Philip Dobree

With grateful thanks to: Jenna Marsh, Jesse Thompson, Rachael Malicki, Tracey Smith, Helen Winfield

Researched photographs ©: J Allan Cash Ltd p.7; Tony Stone Images p.9; Woodmansterne Ltd p.23

Printed in Belgium by Proost

What is light?

In the daytime all of our light comes from the sun. The sun is very bright and hot.

The sun makes more light than anything else. Nothing can make the world light up like the sun.

We can also make our own light. We have lights inside our homes and lights in the streets. We have different coloured lights, and lights that we can carry around with us, like torches and bicycle lights.

On a very **bright** day, we may need to cover our eyes and skin to **protect** them from the **sun**. What would you use?

Warning: never look straight at the sun. It can hurt your eyes, or even make you blind.

When the part of the earth where you live is **facing** the **sun**, it is **daytime**. When the part of the earth where you live is **facing away** from the **sun**, it is **night-time**.

What is dark?

Dark is when there isn't any light. It gets dark at the end of each day. There is less and less light, until we can no longer see the sun, and everywhere around us becomes dark.

The earth turns round and round. This means that every part of the earth spends some of each day facing the sun, and some of each day facing away from the sun. Some of each day is light and some is dark.

Half of the earth is always in darkness, the other half is always in light.

As the part of the earth where you are turns away from the sun, it goes dark. We call this sunset.

What helps us to **see** when it is **dark** outside?

The **light** from the television goes **through** the **glass**. We **can see** the picture behind the glass.

Some of the **light** from the television is **blocked** by the **tissue paper**. We **cannot see** the picture **clearly** behind the tissue paper.

The **cardboard blocks out** all of the **light** from the television. We **cannot see** the picture behind the cardboard.

What can we see through?

We can see through clear things. We can see through a window. This means that we can see things on the other side of a window. It is clear. Light goes through clear things.

Light cannot go through bricks, or wood. They block out all the light. This is why we cannot see through a brick wall or a wooden table.

Some things block out some light, and still let some light through. On a dull day, some of the light from the sun is blocked out by the clouds.

Where there are **clouds**, some of the sunlight is **blocked**. Where there are **no clouds**, the light shines through.

Have you ever seen a **sundial**?

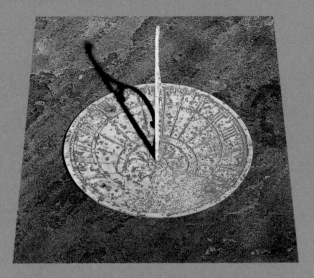

On a **sunny** day, the marker on the sundial casts a **shadow**.

As the **sun moves** across the sky during the day, the **shadow moves** around the sundial.

Sundials can be used to tell the **time**.

How are shadows made?

If you stand with your back to the sun, you will see a darker area on the ground in front of you. This is your shadow.

The light from the sun cannot go through you. Your body is blocking the light from the sun, so that it can't shine on the ground. This is why the shadow has almost the same shape as your body.

What happens to your shadow when you move your body?

In a **dark** room, place a **bright light** so that it shines onto a **white** wall. Holding your hands close to the wall, you can make **finger shadows**. Why is this?

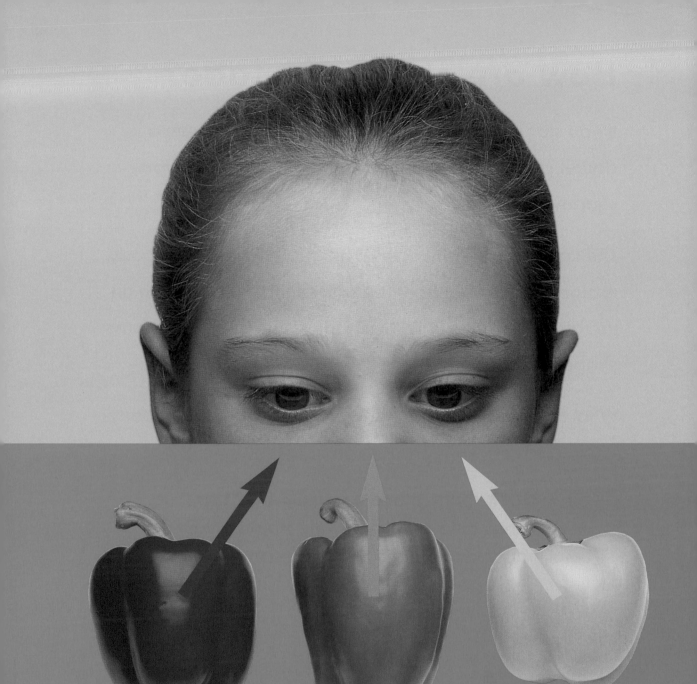

Light shines on the peppers, so
that you can see the **colours**.

Why do things have colour?

Everything around us has a colour. It is light that lets us see colours. This is because light has lots of colours in it. We can see all these colours in a rainbow: red, orange, yellow, green, blue, indigo and violet. By mixing different coloured lights, we can make even more colours.

In the dark, we can't see any colours. This is because there is no light.

If you hold a compact disc towards a light, you will see all the **colours** of the **light** on the disc.

How many **colours** can you see in the peacock feather?

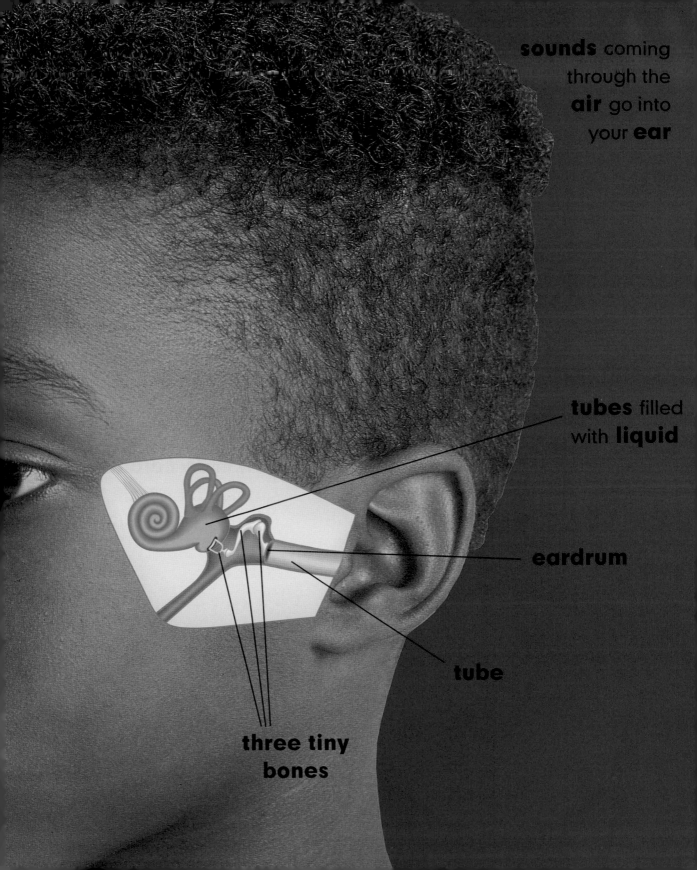

sounds coming through the **air** go into your **ear**

tubes filled with **liquid**

eardrum

tube

three tiny bones

How do we hear sound?

We hear sounds with our ears. Our ears can hear many different kinds of sounds: high and low, quiet and loud. What kinds of sounds do you hear during the day?

You can see part of your ear on the outside of your head. This is your outer ear. The rest of your ear is deep inside your head. This is your inner ear.

The sounds go down a tube from your outer ear to your inner ear. The hole you can see in your ear is the outer end of this tube.

Very **loud sounds** can **hurt** our **ears**. Some people use **ear plugs** or **ear protectors** to **block out** loud sounds.

Never play music too loud. It can make you deaf.

Blow up a **balloon**. Hold the opening gently and let the air out. Can you see the end **moving to and fro**? Listen to the **sound** it makes.

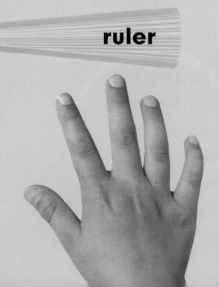

vibrating
alarm clock bells
and hammer

ruler

table

Gently push one end of the **ruler** down, then let it go. What happens to the **sound** if you **move** the ruler?

What is sound?

Sound is something most people can hear.

Sound is made when things vibrate. This is when things move to and fro very quickly. Most of the time this movement is so small and fast that we can't see it.

If you stretch a rubber band and pluck it, it moves to and fro very fast. It moves so fast that you can't see it clearly. While it is moving fast, the rubber band makes a sound. The rubber band is vibrating. When the rubber band stops moving, the sound stops.

Can you **see** and **hear** the **vibration** of a rubber band? If you stretch the band to different lengths, what happens to the sound?

Make a 'telephone' with yoghurt pots and a piece of string. The **sound travels** along the **string** from the speaker to the listener.

Fill a balloon with **water**. **Listen** while someone **speaks** with their lips against the balloon or **taps** the balloon with their fingers. The **sound travels** from the speaker, **through** the **water**, to the listener. How does it sound?

What can we hear?

When you speak to someone standing near you in a room, the sound from your voice travels through the air to the other person. They can hear you clearly.

If they stand in another room while you are talking, they will not hear you so clearly. If you whisper, they won't be able to hear you at all. How loud does the person need to speak or shout for the sound to go through the wall?

You can do an experiment using a sound cannon, which you can make. If you hit one end, the sound travels through the air inside the tube and comes out of the pin-sized hole at the other end.

What happens to the **candles**?

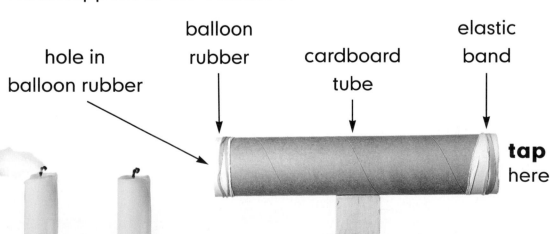

hole in balloon rubber

balloon rubber

cardboard tube

elastic band

tap here

How do we make echoes?

If you stand in a tunnel, or an empty room, and make a noise, you will hear it being repeated. You will hear your voice again after you have made the sound. This is an echo. The echo is quieter than the sound you made first.

The sound goes from you, through the air, and hits the hard wall. When you throw a ball against a wall, it bounces back to you. Sound bounces off the wall in the same way, and travels back to you through the air. You hear the sound again when it comes to your ears.

The Whispering Gallery is inside the dome of St Paul's Cathedral. Inside this **dome**, you can hear **echoes** even if you **whisper**.

Index
^^^^^^